NANDI'S WORLD

BY CHARMAINE MANETO

ISBN 978-1-77920-688-6

Published By
WING UP PUBLISHING

WING UP
PUBLISHING

www.winguppublishing.com
info@winguppublishing.com

Cover designed by : Diligent Palmer
Illustrated by: Tanaka Ronald

This book belongs to.....................

My superpower is...........................

Hello, my name is Nandi
and I am 5 years old.
I live with my parents
and my baby brother Aya.

This is us, I'm so thankful
for my family.

My brother Aya cries, drinks milk and sleeps all day.

My mother says when I was his age, I used to do the same.

While he is sleeping during the day, I go to school.

My favourite part of the day is when I come back from school because I get to wear my favourite princess dress. I like to look like a princess.

When I look into the mirror, I see a beautiful princess. What do you see when you look at yourself in the mirror?

I do my homework in my princess dress. Homework is easy because everything I learn, see, speak and hear at school goes into my brain.

My brain keeps everything because it is a storage. I can use my brain to remember things.

After I do my homework, I help my mama feed and put Aya to sleep. While Aya is sleeping I get some time to play.

This is my dog Brownies, I named him that because he is brown in colour.

I sometimes play with him, he is always so friendly and loves to wag his tail.

While I play, I start to imagine...
I can use my brain to imagine great
things.

I imagine my world. I imagine what
I will be when I grow up.
A ballerina? An engineer? A pilot?
A doctor, maybe even the president.

I wish I could fly. I always imagine
myself in an aeroplane high
up in the sky. Going from one
country to another.

I imagine my world.
My brain is my world.
Welcome to my world.

What do you want your world to
look like? You can imagine
and create it first in your brain.
Whatever you imagine you have
the power to create

After playing, I love to help mama with the dishes. This teaches me to be smart and responsible.

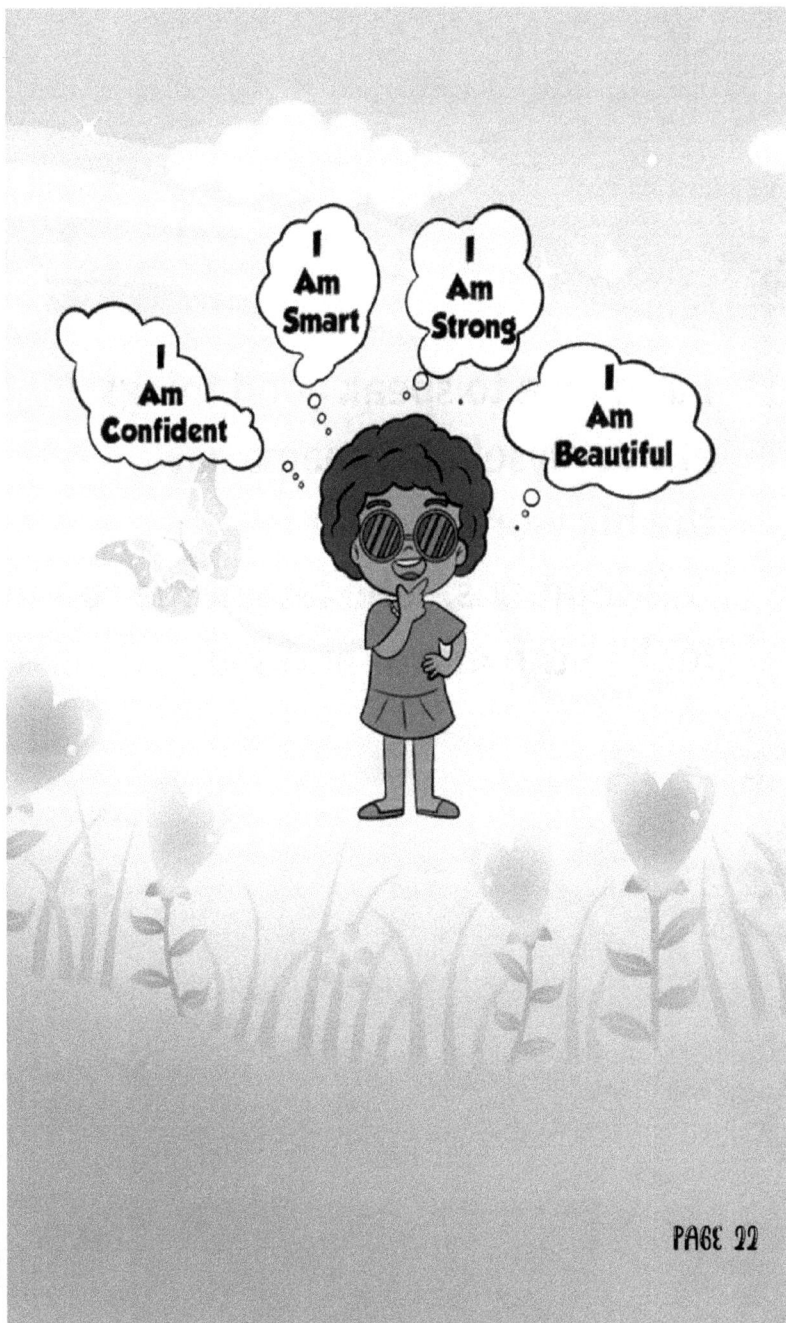

I also love to speak good things about myself. My mama says the big word for that is "affirmations." She taught me to look in the mirror and say:

I AM CONFIDENT; I AM SMART;
I AM STRONG; I AM BEAUTIFUL.

I feel so self-confident after doing it,
you should try it too.

When I go to bed, I put on my pink pyjamas and say a prayer
for my mama, papa, Aya and Brownies.

I hope you enjoyed my world.